FIRST
PEOPLES
of NORTH
AMERICA

THE PEOPLE AND CULTURE OF THE
TLINGIT

ERIKA EDWARDS
RAYMOND BIAL

Cavendish
Square
New York

Published in 2017 by Cavendish Square Publishing, LLC
243 5th Avenue, Suite 136, New York, NY 10016

Copyright © 2017 by Cavendish Square Publishing, LLC

First Edition

Library of Congress Cataloging-in-Publication Data

Names: Edwards, Erika, author. | Bial, Raymond, author.
Title: The people and culture of the Tlingit / Erika Edwards and Raymond Bial.
Description: New York : Cavendish Square Publishing, [2017] |
Series: First peoples of North America | Includes bibliographical references and index.
Identifiers: LCCN 2016038578 (print) | LCCN 2016038976 (ebook) |
ISBN 9781502622518 (library bound) | ISBN 9781502622525 (E-book)
Subjects: LCSH: Tlingit Indians--Juvenile literature. |
Tlingit Indians--Social life and customs--Juvenile literature. |
Indians of North America--Alaska--Juvenile literature.
Classification: LCC E99.T6 E39 2017 (print) | LCC E99.T6 (ebook) |
DDC 979.8004/9727--dc23
LC record available at https://lccn.loc.gov/2016038578

Editorial Director: David McNamara
Editor: Kristen Susienka
Copy Editor: Rebecca Rohan
Associate Art Director: Amy Greenan
Production Coordinator: Karol Szymczuk
Photo Research: J8 Media

ACKNOWLEDGMENTS

We would like to thank all involved in the researching, editing, and photo taking of this book. In particular, Cavendish Square Publishing, for making this book a reality, and our families, for their constant support and encouragement on this writing journey.

CONTENTS

A Tlingit man wears traditional clothing, including a ceremonial headpiece.

AUTHORS' NOTE

At the dawn of the twentieth century, Native Americans were thought to be a vanishing race. However, despite four hundred years of warfare, deprivation, and disease, Native Americans have not gone away. Countless thousands have lost their lives, but over the course of the twentieth century the populations of Native tribes grew tremendously. Even as Native Americans struggle to adapt to modern Western life, they have also kept the flame of their traditions alive—the language, religion, stories, and the everyday ways of life. An exhilarating renaissance in Native American culture is now sweeping the nation from coast to coast.

The First Peoples of North America books depict the social and cultural life of the major nations, from the early history of Native peoples in North America to their present-day struggles for survival and dignity. Historical and contemporary photographs of traditional subjects, as well as period illustrations, are blended throughout each book so that readers may gain a sense of family life in a tipi, a hogan, a longhouse, or in houses today.

No single book can comprehensively portray the intricate and varied lifeways of an entire tribe, or nation. We only hope that young people will come away with a deeper appreciation for the rich tapestry of Native culture—both then and now—and a keen desire to learn more about these first Americans.

The Tlingit settled in an area with tough weather, mountains, and glaciers.

(Yeh) shugu tqit'a da.

That's the way it is.

—Tlingit expression

A CULTURE BEGINS

Practically every culture, race, and people has a legend explaining how they came to be and how they ended up where they are. This is called an origin story. These stories are sometimes passed down orally, written down, or are depicted through works of art. Separately, there are historical facts that explain how people came to be where they are. For the Tlingit (TLING-git) people, these stories begin during a time when people first began migrating to the western hemisphere.

Journey from the Sea

As with other Native Americans, the exact origins of the Tlingit are unknown. However, two theories exist. The most widely held theory is that the Tlingit originally migrated from Asia across a land bridge where the Bering Sea is today. Another theory is that they were originally from Polynesia and arrived in North America by hopping from island to island. It is believed that some Tlingit, whose original name means "human beings" or "people of the tides," have inhabited the shores and interior of southeastern Alaska for thousands of years. People entered the territory of the Tlingit at least ten thousand years ago. About five thousand years ago, these people began to settle in the coastal region. Most probably came from the south. The Tlingit possibly came from camps on the Nass, Skeena, Stikine, and Taku Rivers. They tended to move from south to north and from the coast to the interior, with some families moving upstream as well. In the eighteenth century, large numbers of Haida, another tribe, also pushed into the region and displaced many southern Tlingit people. The earliest known Tlingit villages date from 1200 to 1700 CE. However, according to Tlingit stories, these settlements vanished when they were destroyed by glaciers in the seventeenth and eighteenth centuries. It is believed that some Tlingit also migrated from the interior when glaciers began to nearly block the rivers. These travelers had to pass under massive ice bridges that have since melted away.

The Tlingit have long fascinated visitors to their territory—from the first Russian adventurers of 1741

New Archangel (now known as Sitka, Alaska) was settled by the Russians in the early 1800s. The Russians were the first Europeans to trade with the Tlingit.

to present-day anthropologists. Early explorers found a complex society, rich in art and elaborate tradition, unlike that of other Native people living on the coast. Unrelated to any of the tribes around them, the Tlingit spoke a language that was only vaguely similar to that of the Athapaskan-speaking peoples who had long dominated the interior regions of Alaska and western Canada. The Tlingit also shared a few customs with Athapaskan peoples, having traded with them for centuries. The Tlingit and the Haida were often thought to be related, but the Haida only moved into the region from the Queen Charlotte Islands a little over two hundred years ago.

Different Groups

The Tlingit were composed of three principal groups: Gulf Coast, Northern, and Southern. These three groups all shared a common language and customs.

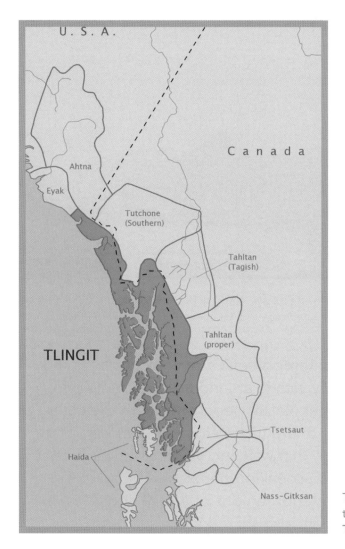

This map shows the territory of the Tlingit in Alaska.

The Gulf Coast Tlingit included the Hoonah of Lituya Bay; the Dry Bay Tlingit at the mouth of the Alsek River; and the Yakutat, who included Tlingit-speaking Eyak people from the Italio River to Icy Bay. In 1910, the Yakutat and Dry Bay Tlingit united as a people. The Northern Tlingit included the Hoonah on the north shore of Cross Sound, Chilkat, Chilkoot, Auk, and Taku; the Sumdum on the mainland; and the Sitka and Hutsnuwu, or Angoon, on the outer islands and coast.

The Southern Tlingit were composed of the Kake, Kuiu, Henya, and Klawock on the islands; the Stikine, or Wrangell; the Tongass; and the Sanya, or Cape Fox, who lived on the mainland or coastal harbors. In addition, there is a small group of Tlingit-speaking people living in inland British Columbia and adjacent Yukon Territory whose culture is partly Tlingit and partly Athapaskan. This book is mainly about the Tlingit proper, sometimes called Coastal Tlingit to distinguish themselves from these Inland Tlingit, who are believed to have had Athapaskan ancestors.

Tlingit neighbors to the south were the Tsimshian, while the Haida lived to the southeast, and various Athapaskan groups inhabited the interior on the east. To the north lived the Eyak, a coastal people whose language belonged to the Athapaskan family. As mentioned above, some of the Eyak people became Tlingit speakers and united with the Yakutat, the northernmost of the Tlingit groups.

A Culture of Land and Water

The Tlingit have long made their home on a narrow strip of land known as the Alaskan panhandle, which stretches from Icy Bay in the north to Chatham Strait in the south. The land varies from misty tidewater to lofty, snowcapped mountains. At the northern end of Tlingit territory, along the Gulf of Alaska coast, there are few bays and other sheltered places for landing **canoes**. But to the south, an archipelago of windswept islands, just 30 miles (48 kilometers) wide and 500 miles (805 km) long, protects most of the shoreline from the battering waves of the ocean. It is a region of rolling waves, mountainous islands, and rugged coastline shaped long ago by numerous glaciers and fjords. Several rivers, notably the Stikine, Taku, Chilkat, and Alsek, cut through the jagged mountains, providing water routes to the interior.

Thrust upward by the continental plates, the rocky land is blanketed in the north with lush rain forests of spruce, hemlock, and yellow cedar trees, and in the south with red cedar. These forests tower over a dense, tangled undergrowth abounding in blueberries. There are few temperature extremes; both winters and summers are relatively mild. Clouds often hang over the treetops, rain descends like a veil, and fog drifts low over the waters. The coast is drenched in rain for two hundred to two hundred sixty days a year with total rainfall ranging from 100 to 220 inches (254 to 559 centimeters), making the region the wettest in North America. During late autumn and winter, strong winds and snow occasionally swirl into the river valleys and blast the interior.

The waters of the Pacific Ocean teemed with sea mammals—harbor seals, fur seals, and sea otters, along with whales and porpoises. Traditionally, the Tlingit caught an abundance of fish, especially halibut, salmon, and herring. In early spring, people caught candlefish, also known as eulachon or hooligan.

As the weather warmed, the salmon began to run. The Tlingit caught five different kinds of salmon from midsummer until late autumn, when the rivers began to freeze over. Most of the salmon were dried and stored for the long, lean months of winter. At low tide, the Tlingit gathered shellfish and seaweed that had washed onto the beach. During the spring and summer, ducks and other waterfowl migrated up the Pacific flyway. They nested or paused in the region, providing the Tlingit with eggs and meat. For fur and flesh, the Tlingit hunted a variety of wild animals—wolves, moose, black-tailed deer, Dall sheep, and mountain goats. There were also marten, beaver, and mink. Black bears and grizzly bears ranged throughout the ancestral Tlingit territory. The grizzlies along the coastal rivers became huge as they feasted on salmon, while smaller grizzlies fed on plants and animals farther inland.

The Tlingit crafted canoes such as this one. Canoe travel became essential to coastal life. Today, the Tlingit still make and use their own canoes.

The Tlingit looked to the land and the water to provide themselves with food and the materials with which they made their clothing, belongings, and works of art. In the forests, they cut towering red cedar trees into logs from which they carved impressive **totem poles**. They also formed posts, beams, and wide planks for building their **clan houses**. They shaped the boards into **bentwood boxes**, crafted graceful canoes, and made other essential tools.

Because of the rugged terrain, people usually traveled by water among the scattered islands. Long before the arrival of Europeans, they paddled canoes, often for hundreds of miles, to wage war on enemies, trade with allies, and visit neighbors for lavish ceremonies known as **potlatches**.

Creation Origins of the Tlingit

No one knows when the Tlingit first settled along the coast of southeastern Alaska. According to some stories, they journeyed there from the headwaters of the Nass River countless generations ago. This region of British Columbia, just outside of the Tlingit territory, features in many of their origin stories. One tale recounts the activities of a great bird, Raven, at the source of the Nass River. Revered among the Tlingit, Raven could be a trickster, but he often helped people, as illustrated in the following story:

> No one knows just how the story of Raven began, only that the mischievous trickster has always existed. He was even here long ago, when there was no light in the world. At that time, a rich man kept the light to himself in a large clan house far up the Nass River.
>
> Raven was very clever and he wondered what he could do to bring light to the world. He finally came up with a plan. He made himself

very small—as tiny as a speck of dust—and dropped into a stream near the man's home. The man's daughter drank from the stream, and magically, she became heavy with child.

The rich man wondered how his daughter had become pregnant, yet he was overjoyed that he would soon have a grandchild. When the daughter went into labor, she lay down in a bed of plush furs. But the baby refused to be born on such finery. So, the people in the clan house spread moss to make a humble bed, and there the infant was born. His eyes were very bright as he glanced around.

The child grew rapidly and soon began to crawl around the clan house. The wealthy man was so pleased to have a grandson he did not question why the child was growing so fast.

One day, the child noticed three bentwood boxes of varying sizes and shapes hanging upon the walls. Pointing to the wooden boxes, the child wailed day after day. At last, the grandfather said to his daughter, "Give my grandson the box hanging on the end. That is the box of stars."

The box was taken down and given to the child, who played happily. Rolling the box on the floor, he gradually moved toward the center of the clan house until he was under the smoke hole. Suddenly, he opened the box, releasing the stars, which rose through the smoke hole and ascended into the night sky. The stars quickly scattered throughout the heavens, just as they are today.

Some days later, the child began to cry with such anguish that people thought that he might die. The grandfather finally said to his daughter, "Untie the next box and give it to him."

The child played with the box under the smoke hole. After a while, he opened the box and the moon floated up through the smoke hole, high into the sky.

Just one bentwood box remained—the one that held sunlight. The child now cried for this box. As he glanced around the clan house, his eyes changed colors and people began to suspect that he was not an ordinary little boy.

Yet a grandfather loves his grandchild as much as he does his own daughter. So, the grandfather said to his daughter, "Give it to him."

When the child had the box in his hands, he uttered the raven cry, "Ka!", and flew up through the smoke hole, carrying the sun with him. The world was suddenly flooded with light.

The rich man realized that Raven had only pretended to be his grandson. He shouted, "Raven has tricked me. He has taken all of my things."

And that is how Raven brought the light of the stars, moon, and sun into the world.

The Alaskan landscape provided beautiful scenery and ample terrain on which to build communities.

Regardless of their origins, the Tlingit have developed into a strong culture with a rich history. Their communities and identities have changed and been challenged over the generations, yet they continue with pride and determination.

The Tlingit depended on the land and resources around them to form a strong civilization.

Yan tután, aagáa yéi kgwatee.

Have faith and it shall be so.

—Tlingit expression

BUILDING
A
CIVILIZATION

After the Tlingit arrived in the western hemisphere, they had to build and grow a civilization. In order to do so, they established laws and family organizational rules. They also created communal buildings and dwellings. These building blocks produced an environment that allowed them to thrive in their new homeland.

Tlingit villages, called kwan, had large structures for gathering the community together and smaller ones in which people lived.

The People and Culture of the Tlingit

Kwan

The Tlingit lived in groups or villages known as **kwan**. The people in each kwan made their homes in the same geographic region, where they intermarried and lived peacefully with each other. There may have been fifteen to twenty kwan when the Tlingit first encountered European explorers. Communities where many Tlingit gathered often had "kwan" in the name—Sitka-kwan, Taku-kwan, Heeny-kwan, and so forth. Today, Ketchikan, Juneau, Wrangell, and other cities of southeastern Alaska are located on the village sites of several traditional kwan.

In each kwan's region, there was at least one main village, often situated on a sheltered cove. It was ideally located near hunting grounds, berry patches, clam beds, deep water for halibut, and other food sources. The village had to be near fresh water, stands of timber, and trails or streams that led into the interior. If the community was also located near a salmon river, the people might live there year-round. However, most Tlingit lived in the village only during the winter, then they abandoned it in the summer for fishing and hunting camps. As cold weather set in, they returned to the winter village.

The village consisted of a row of large plank houses facing the beach. People often built walls called palisades around their houses or occasionally around the entire village. Sometimes, wealthy **nobles** constructed a fort nearby where they could defend themselves against invaders. Canoes were usually pushed up onto the beach in front of the house and kept under mats or shelters. Throughout the village stood **smokehouses** and drying racks for preserving fish. Small houses on poles and plank-lined pits were used for storing food and belongings. There were also sweat huts and shelters used by the women during menstruation and childbirth. Boxes holding the powerful and sacred objects of the **shaman**, or medicine man, were hidden in the nearby forest, well away from the people in the village.

Tlingit Dwellings and Clan House Living

Large rectangular houses served as both homes and ceremonial buildings. About six families, totaling forty to fifty people, including slaves, lived in each clan house. Four corner posts, elaborately carved and painted with ancestral and totem designs, formed the basic structure, and a ridge beam supported the gently sloping, peaked roof. Thick, wide cedar planks were

Inside a clan house, the Tlingit created space for all. They also decorated the buildings with totem poles, as seen in this photograph.

used to sheath the walls and gabled roof of the clan house. There were no windows in the building—only a small oval doorway. Through openings in the roof, light streamed into the plank house and smoke from cooking fires drifted upward into the sky.

Inside, the earthen floor was dug slightly lower to make two or three levels. The nobles who owned the clan house required their slaves to sleep on the ground by the oval doorway. **Commoners** related to the nobles or who worked for them slept on benches or platforms on one of the lower levels, where they tended their own fires for warmth and cooking. In the middle of the clan house there was a large communal hearth where meals were cooked for the nobles and their guests at celebrations. On the highest level at the back of the clan house the nobles occupied secluded rooms where they slept on wooden platforms. Their small apartments were separated with mats, piles of boxes, or wooden screens carved and painted with **clan** crests. These partitions could be removed to make a large space for ceremonies. Valuable treasures were also hidden away in this space. A platform in front of these rooms was known as the "head of house," or place of honor where the owner and his family sat, guests were received, and the deceased might lie in state. The oldest man of the noble family was usually considered the owner and chief, but his mother and sisters were highly influential members of the household as well.

In the late nineteenth century, carpentry tools, nails, and sawn lumber became available to the Tlingit. Many people who had become wealthy through fishing began to build large frame houses on pilings with modern windows, doors, and iron stoves. Several families lived in each of these houses that they furnished with brass beds, tables, and chairs. Later, the houses were divided into separate, unheated rooms, but people complained that these dwellings were not as warm as the old clan houses. People displayed painted crests on these houses. However, by the 1920s, an influential organization known as the Alaska Native Brotherhood had convinced many people to do away with this practice. Many people are now returning to the traditions of their ancestors, including the painting of crests on their homes.

A Society of Moieties, Clans, and Nobility

The Tlingit believed, and continue to believe, that every individual belongs to one of two **moieties**, or separate halves: Raven and Wolf (sometimes called Eagle in the north). The two moieties were opposites in every aspect of life, including marriage, death, and important ceremonies. Among the Tlingit, everything in daily life and the universe was ordered around the moieties and their relations with each other. Each moiety comprised more than thirty clans, which were further divided into family **lineages**, or house groups of related families, descending from a common ancestor. Members of clans in one moiety had to marry into clans of the other moiety. One could not marry a member of one's own moiety. A Wolf had to marry a Raven, and a Raven had to marry a Wolf.

Tlingit society was also **matrilineal**, which means children traced their descent through the mother's side of the family. Children were always considered part of their mother's family. Throughout life, the mother's brothers played more crucial roles than the father in raising the children because they were more closely related to their sister than her husband. A man also inherited wealth and his social position through his mother's side of the family. Titles, crests, and other privileges were considered hereditary property as well.

The complex society was also hierarchical, with individuals and lineages ranked from commoners to nobility. Upper classes, or nobles, owned the

The People and Culture of the Tlingit

The Tlingit had different moieties named for different animals. The Wolf or Eagle moiety was one example.

Building a Civilization

largest houses and enjoyed the greatest wealth and prominence, along with the rights to hunt and gather near the villages. Commoners had to pay to hunt, fish, or gather in these places. Commoners achieved some respect as artists, such as mask or canoe makers. They could also achieve higher status by becoming shamans. Others were simply considered the lower classes. Many Tlingit owned slaves, who were captives and their children seized in battles with neighboring tribes. Slaves had no rights and were not regarded as part of Tlingit society. They were forced to do the hardest chores around the village. Yet if they proved themselves as craftsmen, hunters, and fishermen, they might someday be freed and respected for their ability. After the United States acquired Alaska in 1867, slaves were liberated and became the lowest members of the social order.

The noble members of a particular clan or family lineage held all territory and property rights, including rights to locations for houses, graves, and camps for fishing, hunting, berry picking, and gathering seaweed. All clan property could be sold, traded, or given away, usually when an owner died, or taken in warfare. Clan and lineage chiefs, or headmen, managed the wealth of their group and directed hunting and fishing activities. They also ordered the death of trespassers and hosted memorial services.

The law was based upon moiety, clan, and house. Any injury to members on the other side had to be resolved by payment of goods, property, or services. If a commoner murdered a chief and could not come up with adequate payment, the chief of his clan might

The People and Culture of the Tlingit

be killed. Occasionally, hostages known as "deer" were exchanged for a period of eight days as proof of earnest intent to settle a dispute peacefully. The "deer" rested quietly, enjoying good food and comforts, as the negotiations were underway. In the case of major disputes, such as a war, a clan might have to give a valuable crest to its opponent.

The Tlingit went to war against other clans or tribes for plunder or revenge. They not only killed their enemies but captured women and children as slaves. Their weapons included bows and arrows, spears, war clubs, and knives. Warriors protected themselves with armor made of hides and wooden rods worn over moose-skin shirts. Upon their return, they celebrated a victory with feasting and dancing.

Crests

Along with personal wealth, each clan owned certain emblems, or pictorial designs, known as "crests." The clan's crest represented its totem, which was usually an animal but might be a heavenly body, a natural feature such as the ocean, or a supernatural being like the thunderbird. Each clan inherited these crests. Many crests were over a thousand years old. Crests honored ancestors and granted special rights to clan members. For example, in one well-known story of Glacier Bay, a careless girl triggered a glacier that destroyed much of her town, and her grandmother had to pay with her own life. Descendants in their clan have since used a glacier as a crest symbol.

The major Raven crest symbols were Raven, Owl, Whale, Sea Lion, Salmon, Frog, Sleep Bird, Big Dipper,

The Tlingit made elaborate robes and clothes with animal and other designs.

The People and Culture of the Tlingit

Sun, Moon, and Ocean. Those of the Wolf, or Eagle, included Wolf, Eagle, Petrel, Bear, Killer Whale, Shark, Halibut, Thunderbird, and others. Crests were prominently featured on canoes, feast dishes, clothing, blankets, drums, rattles, and other cherished objects. People also proudly displayed their crests on totem poles and the house posts that supported the entrance wall of the dwelling. A Tlingit noble who wished to make known his deeds or those of his ancestors carefully selected crest designs. He then hired an artist, who beautifully carved and painted the pole in a style in which a curving black frame outlined each sculpted figure. A totem pole could be placed at the entrance to the noble's home, used to honor the remains of a deceased relative, or raised as a memorial on the beach. When the totem pole was finished, a celebration called a potlatch was held. The guests helped to raise the pole, after which everyone enjoyed a great feast and told many stories about the figures depicted on the towering pole.

In any civilization, it is important to create a set of rules and organizational patterns for people to follow. With a focus on a matrilineal society, clans, and lineage, the Tlingit people were able to establish a way of life that reflected a well-functioning society. Many of the original social and structural concepts and ideas that were produced are still ingrained in the culture of the Tlingit today.

Many Tlingit women continue the tradition of weaving intricate designs on blankets and clothing in the Chilkat style.

CHAPTER THREE

Yakíei ·y·, woosht kanAx wutoowda.aadi.

It is very good that we have all come together.

—Tlingit phrase

LIFE IN A TLINGIT VILLAGE

The Tlingit had many different rituals and celebrations according to the season. In the spring, people hunted, fished, and gathered seaweed. In warmer months, they ventured nearer shore to hunt seals. During the summer and the fall, they caught salmon in the rivers and streams, hunted otters, and dug wild potatoes. As the cold of winter approached, they returned to their winter villages, where they held potlatches and traded for goods. For many years, each generation followed similar cycles, forming tradition.

Cycle of Life

The Tlingit life cycle focused on moving through major life events. A Tlingit would come of age and then assume the responsibilities of his or her family and then the tribe. Many rituals of the Tinglit relate to the rites of passage at the various stages of life.

Being Born

The Tlingit thought that infants were the reincarnation of relatives on the mother's side of the family, who would carry on the name of her family lineage and clan. They believed that babies often remembered people and events from their previous life. Between death and rebirth, one "was ashes." The Tlingit regarded a person as a number of layers around a core of mind, soul, and emotions. The outer body had eight parts, counted by doubling the number of upper and lower limbs—four for the arms and four for the legs.

When a woman was about to give birth, she was accompanied to a bark shelter by two or more experienced women, often her husband's sisters, who helped to deliver the baby. They were later paid well for their assistance. The mother and her newborn remained in the shelter for about ten days to avoid contaminating the clan house and its inhabitants.

Growing Up

When a boy turned seven or eight years old, he went to live with one of his mother's brothers to begin his

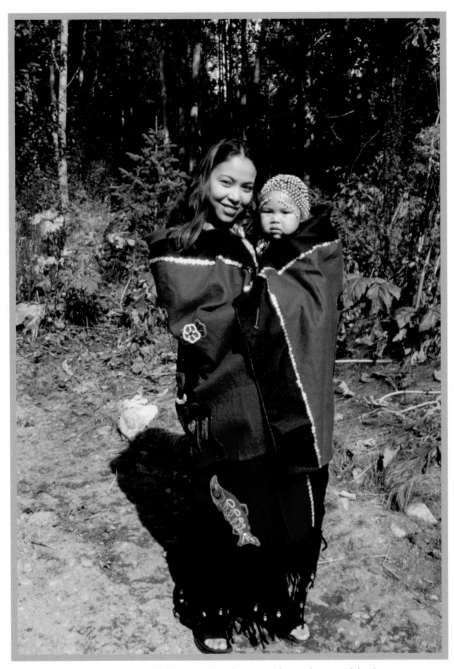

A Tlingit mother and her child snuggle close in a large button blanket.

Life in a Tlingit Village

education. The uncle taught the young man about his family heritage and his responsibilities to his clan and lineage—especially if the uncle was a house owner or chief and the boy was his heir. Under his uncle's guidance, the boy toughened and purified himself by plunging into icy water in the morning, whipping his own body, chopping piles of firewood, and undertaking other vigorous tasks. From his uncle, the boy learned the many rituals and beliefs, as well as the practical skills, involved in fishing and hunting. Until he killed his first game, a young man could eat only certain foods. He came of age when he brought home his prey. A great feast was then held in his honor, after which he was regarded as a "master of game."

Mothers took primary responsibility for educating and training their daughters. They instructed them in their important roles in their families and the community. Tlingit women generally enjoyed high status, mostly because they were responsible for the arduous work of drying and smoking the fish that sustained everyone in the village. So, it was essential that a mother properly teach her daughter the many skills and tasks that she would need to provide for her family and manage a household. These included cooking meals, making clothing, and caring for the children. Until she had her first period, a girl also had to abstain from certain foods, a practice through which she learned the importance of sacrifice and discipline.

Maturing

A girl came of age when she had her first period. At this time, she was confined in a dark room or cellar in the clan house for at least eight days, but often much longer, depending on her rank and wealth. A high-ranking girl might be secluded for two years. During the girl's seclusion, her father's sister, who represented his lineage, closely supervised her, while her mother and grandmother instructed her in the traditions of their house.

During her seclusion, the young woman also performed many rituals and observed many restrictions to assure prosperity in the future. For example, to avoid contaminating herself, she could touch herself only with a scratcher. She washed her hair in blackberry juice and wore a black feather cap, believing that her hair would keep its dark color in old age. For the first eight days of seclusion, she ate and drank nothing except a little water on the fourth and eighth day. If she reached eagerly for the drink, it was thrown away so that she would learn self-control. At the end of her eight-day fast, her maternal relatives held a feast. At this time, her dolls were given away to paternal cousins. During the remainder of her two-year seclusion, the young woman was not allowed to eat fresh fish, shellfish, or seaweed. She ate only from her own dishes. If she glanced at the sky, it was believed that there would be storms, so she had to wear a hood draped with strings of dentalia shells.

At the end of her seclusion, the young woman was bathed and then dressed in new clothes. She was adorned with gold bracelets and other jewelry. She emerged from the room or cellar with a pale complexion that was much admired. However, because of her inactivity, her legs had become so weak that she could barely stand or walk more than a few steps. Her lower lip was pierced for a piece of jewelry known as a labret. Families of high status also gave a potlatch to thank her paternal aunts for their devoted efforts. These aunts then presented the young woman as ready to be married.

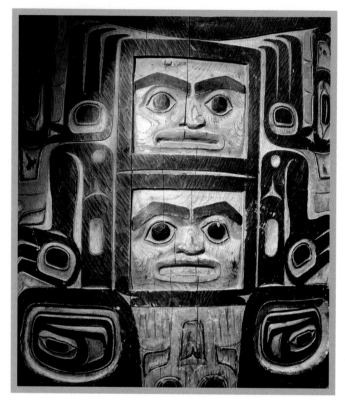

The figures on this carved board symbolize ancestry and social status. Boards like this would be attached to posts inside the home.

Marrying

Any man and woman of opposite moieties could marry each other, but in high-ranking families, marriages were often arranged. Ideally, couples were of equal rank so that their marriage would strengthen the bonds between houses and clans. Marriages of nobles, in particular, served to build and maintain alliances between families.

During the marriage ceremony, the fathers of the young man and woman exchanged gifts, often valuable crest objects. Some marriages were arranged to obtain such wealth. A rich man whose gifts were accepted then took his bride home. However, a common man unable to provide sufficient gifts had to remain in the home of the bride and work for the father-in-law as a form of payment, or "bride price."

A man might be married to two or more sisters at the same time. If his wife died, he was entitled to marry her younger sister or another close relative. Few women had more than one husband, but a widow was expected to marry her husband's brother or maternal nephew. Although these marriages united families and clans, they often matched couples of very unequal age. When a young man or woman had to take a much older person as a mate, a related young person was also designated as "future wife" or "future husband" to take the place of the older spouse upon his or her death.

Dying

When a man, woman, or child died, the rites varied widely according to the rank and lineage of the deceased. There was an elaborate ceremony when a noble or house or clan chief passed away. A lavish funeral ended with a great memorial potlatch in which the successor inherited his wealth and position. When a shaman died, special rituals were observed. The widow and mourners did not cut their hair, and his body was not cremated. It was placed in a small house or cave, along with some of his sacred objects and the image of a spirit guardian. In contrast, the bodies of slaves were

The Tlingit were known for their detailed carvings, like this potlatch bowl.

thrown onto the beach to be washed away in the sea or devoured by scavengers.

When a nobleman died, there were usually eight days of mourning. Clan members gathered to sing four mourning songs and make donations to pay for the funeral. Men of the opposite moiety—especially those married to the deceased's sisters—prepared the body and made all the arrangements, including the wake and cremation. Similarly, the body of a deceased woman was attended by her husband's sisters. With his body adorned in ceremonial clothes and his face painted with clan designs, the deceased was propped up at the head of the house, with his wealth piled around him.

The wake continued for eight days, although the time might be longer for a chief. Mourners wore old clothes with ropes tied around their waists. They cut their hair or later burned it at the cremation. Widows observed especially harsh rituals, such as fasting, to express their grief. After four days, the body was taken out of the house through an opening made by removing a plank from the wall. It was carried to a pyre and cremated while mourners sang four more songs and the women of the widow's family, wrapped in button blankets, swayed to the music. Valuables of the deceased were thrown into the fire. It was believed that burning the body released the soul, which then departed the village through the forest before climbing a mountain to "the other side." Afterward, members of the opposite clan gathered the ashes and bones in a blanket and placed them in a grave box or mortuary totem pole.

After the funeral, the widow and other mourners bathed and put on new clothing. They burned all their old garments. That evening, the mourners held a potlatch for the opposite moiety to show their gratitude. The widow or widower was expected to remarry a member of that house or clan after a year of mourning.

To honor the deceased, many Tlingit, especially those living in the south, traditionally raised tall, carved, and painted mortuary poles near their homes. Those living in the north tended to keep the ashes in boxes painted with clan crests or covered with a valuable Chilkat blanket and placed high on poles. Over time, the Tlingit did not raise these grave boxes. In the late nineteenth century, through Christian influence, the Tlingit began to bury their dead. They built a small house on the grave with doors and glass windows through which one could view the cherished belongings of the deceased. Over time, the houses were replaced by cement slabs, and the graves were often fenced. The Tlingit also came to use marble tombstones on which crest symbols were carved. In recent years, they have added Christian inscriptions and images.

Feeding a Community

The Tlingit fished and hunted for survival, yet they also believed that every creature had a soul. No animal—not even the smallest bird—was killed needlessly or wasted. Instead of attempting to dominate the wilderness, a hunter respected his prey. Before a hunt, he observed a number of strict rituals. He purified himself by fasting and bathing. He did not speak of the game he sought, especially bears, since it was thought that these powerful animals could hear what was said of them. His wife and children also had to remain silent until his return because any inappropriate utterance or action might influence the hunt, change the weather, or bring misfortune, even death. The hunter also relied on magical amulets. He departed before dawn and fasted during his pursuit of game. He might carry a dried salmon in the event of an emergency, but it was generally believed that he would hunt better if the animals knew that he was hungry. After he made a kill, he prayed to the dead body and spirit of the animal. He explained his need for its flesh and begged to be forgiven. Raising his voice in song, he thanked the animal for having given its life. He might also make an offering of eagle down. He returned the vital parts, such as the head, bones, and certain organs, to the water, or burned them, to ensure that the animal would be reincarnated.

This handmade fishhook was used to catch different fish from the rivers, streams, and oceans near Tlingit communities.

Men hunted many kinds of land animals, often with the help of dogs. Bears were trapped in deadfalls and snares, shot with bows and arrows, or most often with spears. For hunting and for warfare, men made 6- to 8-foot (1.8- to 2.4-meter) spears of spruce or hemlock shafts. Most often, hunters pursued bears in the early spring, when their fur was in prime condition for making robes. Three or four dogs either roused a bear from a den or tracked and held the animal at bay until the hunters arrived for the kill. For hunting deer, mountain goats, Dall sheep, and other animals, men used bows of yew or hemlock and arrows of yellow cedar. Spears and arrows were fitted with a sharp blade of slate, copper, and in later years, iron. In ancient times, men also hunted with whip slings and darts. Young men ventured above the timberline to hunt deer while older men ordered their well-trained dogs to chase the

INGREDIENTS

Pastry:

2 cups all-purpose flour

½ cup vegetable oil

3 tablespoons cold water

Filling:

½ pound halibut, cut into 1-inch cubes

2 cups cooked rice

½ cup onions, chopped

2 hard-boiled eggs, chopped

½ teaspoon salt

½ teaspoon pepper

RECIPE

FISH PIE

Preheat oven to 350 degrees Fahrenheit. Add oil to flour and mix well with a fork. Sprinkle 3 tablespoons of cold water over pastry and mix well. Divide pastry in half and form into balls. Roll each ball into flat circles about 11 inches in diameter. Fit one circle of pastry dough into a pie pan and trim any excess from the edges. Spread 1 cup cooked rice in pie pan. Place halibut cubes on the rice, then layer with onions and eggs, followed by the second cup of rice. Cover with the other circle of dough, crimping along the edge.

Make several slits in the dough as steam vents. Bake 30 to 35 minutes or until the crust is golden brown.

You may substitute fresh or canned salmon for the halibut in this recipe.

animals down to the shore where they could be shot from canoes. Dogs also drove mountain goats and Dall sheep to the hunters. They killed these animals for their fat, their horns—which were used to make spoons and feast dishes—and their wool, which was woven into clothing. Tlingit people who lived inland hunted caribou, moose, and occasionally wood bison.

The Tlingit speared or netted beaver under the ice. They caught ducks, geese, and other waterfowl, often with skillfully placed snares. These birds were sought not only for their succulent meat but also for their feathers and beaks, which were used to decorate clothing. However, they never hunted land otters. It was believed that people who had drowned or died in the woods were reincarnated as these animals. It was also believed that when a shaman died, his spirit most often assumed the form of a land otter.

The Tlingit relied heavily on fish as a source of food, especially on five kinds of salmon—king (chinook), pink (humpback), silver (coho), red (sockeye), and chum (dog salmon). In late spring, they moved to their fishing camps where they remained until fall, except for some winter villages that were already located on salmon rivers. Some of the fish were boiled, baked, or roasted. However, the women, helped by slaves, sun-dried or cured the salmon in smokehouses and then wrapped most of the fish in bales for the winter. Salmon caught late in the season were often frozen whole during the cold weather.

The Tlingit employed a variety of clever methods for harvesting salmon. Most were caught in boxlike traps made of wooden slats placed across an opening in a weir. People living on the Chilkat River also used funnel-shaped traps for salmon and eulachon. On tidal streams, men sometimes made stone walls on which they piled branches. When the tide fell, salmon became trapped and were easily caught. In August, when water levels became low, the Tlingit placed a row of sharp stakes across the mouth of a river. As they tried to swim upstream, the salmon impaled themselves on the stakes and were gathered. The Tlingit also caught salmon with harpoons or spears fitted with barbed points of antler, bone, or copper—the same kind they used to kill seals, sea lions, sea otters, and porpoises.

In the rivers and sea around them, the Tlingit caught trout, cod, rock cod, herring, and halibut with hooks and lines made from animal gut. Some fishermen also trolled for salmon using herring as bait. To catch halibut in deep waters, they devised a large, ingenious fish hook of yellow cedar and alder wood with a sharp barb made of bone, and later of iron. They used a piece of octopus as bait, a stone as a sinker, and an inflated seal stomach or a wood figure of a bird as a float. Halibut might weigh as much as 100 pounds (45 kilograms), and fishermen faced a daunting task in hauling in a large, thrashing fish without capsizing their boat. To catch herring, a man standing in the bow of a canoe dragged a rake of thirty to fifty sharp bones or nails through the school of fish, impaling several fish at once. Herring were prized for their flesh and oil, but especially for their **roe**. Men also placed hemlock branches in shallow water where the herring **spawned**, then came back to collect their eggs. During spring and summer runs, they also caught candlefish in dip nets or in funnel traps. These small fish were valued for their delicious meat and rich oil. The fish had so much oil that people inserted a twisted spruce bark wick in them and burned the fish as candles.

The Tlingit depended on the ocean for many other foods. At low tide, they gathered seaweed and caught shellfish along the beach. They also hunted many kinds of sea mammals for their flesh and fur, notably harbor seals, fur seals, sea lions, sea otters, and porpoises. Unlike the Haida and other coastal tribes, they rarely hunted whales, and only the bravest men attempted to kill a sea lion. Yet this animal's thick hide was valued for making heavy cords and ropes. Paddling along in their canoes, they most often speared otters and seals with harpoons. They rendered the seals' blubber into oil, ate the otters' meat, and fashioned the plush furs of both animals into warm clothing.

Women and children also gathered berries, such as blueberries, elderberries, wild strawberries, and highbush cranberries. These were eaten fresh or preserved by cooking and shaping into cakes that were dried or stored in wooden boxes filled with oil. The Tlingit also enjoyed the sweet inner bark of hemlock trees. During the early spring, they harvested the tender shoots of salmonberries, angelica, and cow parsnips. In spring and fall, they dug roots, especially fern, rice root, and wild sweet potatoes.

Because of the rocky landscape and chilly weather, the Tlingit did not typically cultivate crops. However, in the early nineteenth century, people at Angoon and Killisnoo became well known for growing small potatoes, which they most likely acquired from the Russians who had settled there. At one time, the Tlingit also grew tobacco, which was dried and mixed with yellow cedar ashes and lime from crushed and roasted seashells. Mixing the tobacco with spruce or cedar gum, they made pellets that were sucked for their flavor. After the Russians introduced leaf tobacco and pipes, the Tlingit made ornately carved pipes, often with crest symbols, and smoked at funerals. Yet women still used **tobacco pellets** until around 1900.

Preparing Food from the Land and Water

Fresh deer meat—especially the liver—was prized by the Tlingit. Meat was often slightly cooked or smoked, then preserved in oil or stored in a box with fat poured over the contents. Women skillfully cut salmon and halibut so thinly that the flesh could be easily dried, smoked, and tied into bundles. Salmon heads and eggs were fermented and eaten as a delicacy like rich cheese. The Tlingit also cooked salmon eggs, often with black seaweed or berries.

Oil was rendered from salmon heads, eulachon, herring, seal blubber, and mountain goat fat. Better grease was obtained from rancid fish and seal fat, so the fish were first left in a pit and blubber was kept in a sealskin bag for several days. To render fat, especially from candlefish, the Tlingit used a canoe as a large pot. They filled the canoe with water and fish, and brought the water to a boil by adding hot rocks. The oil was released from the fish into the water and was then strained into boxes. Any remaining oil was squeezed from the fish by hand or by sitting on them.

Kindling a fire with a red cedar hand drill or iron pyrite and quartz strikers, women baked foods in earthen ovens lined with leaves or boiled them in watertight boxes or baskets filled with heated rocks. They made spoons and dippers from hardwood or the horns of sheep and goats. They served food on wooden platters and dishes with basketry cups and woven mats. Feast utensils were elaborately adorned with crest emblems and inlaid with abalone shell. Baskets, bags, and boxes were used for storage, the finest of which were bentwood boxes with tightly fitting corners and lids, and spruce root baskets woven with striking geometric designs of dyed grass and fern stems.

Tlingit Carving

The Tlingit were highly skilled at many handicrafts, including beadwork and basketry. However, from ancient times to the present day, they have been most renowned as carvers. The striking, carved designs traditionally portrayed animals, either realistically or in a highly stylized form. Totem poles and many other carved objects were usually painted in the traditional blue-green and red colors of the Tlingit. Often, the animals' features—notably the eyes, fins, feathers, or joints—were traced by bold, curving, black lines.

Talented artists made many kinds of objects, ranging in shape and size from amulets to totem poles. They carved goat and sheep horns into impressive feasting spoons. They hammered gold and silver coins, as well as native copper, into distinctive shapes that they then carved. Carvers emphasized objects that reflected deeply held beliefs and enhanced ceremonies. Masks, rattles, and staffs were carved and painted for potlatch dances and songs and for the healing rituals undertaken by shamans. Ornately carved bowls and eating utensils were displayed only at potlatches, while those for everyday meals were more simply adorned. Carvers made bentwood boxes for storing food and clothing as well. They also crafted watertight boxes for cooking soups and stews. These boxes were not placed over a fire; instead, hot stones were dropped into the boxes to bring the water to a boil. Large partition screens were exquisitely carved, often with a family crest.

Carvers worked with ivory, antler, and bone, but most often they worked with wood. Surrounded by lush rain forests, the Tlingit lived in the midst of an abundance of timber. For carving totem poles, they used red and yellow cedar. These woods have a straight grain, which splits evenly, making them excellent choices for clan house planks as well. Alder was traditionally preferred for dishes and eating utensils, since this wood does not affect the flavor of the food. Today, some carvers also work with birch, which has a lovely grain.

Carving tools included **adzes**, axes, drills, and knives. These tools and blades originally were made of stone, bone, or shell. In the late eighteenth century, the Tlingit began to forge iron tools. They acquired the metal through trade or salvaged iron from shipwrecks. Carvers turned the point of a drill to make a hole through which they sewed or tied pieces of wood together. They used many kinds of adzes to carefully shape pieces of wood. Sharp knives of many shapes and sizes were designed to snugly fit the hand of the carver, allowing him to give purposeful form to the wood.

Explorers on the Northwest coast were struck by the house posts and totem poles that towered over Native villages like cedar monuments at the edge of the sea. Carved with figures of animals and people, some of these poles were 90 feet (27 m) tall. Totems of animals such as a bear, eagle, or killer whale were carved in the wood and painted. Poles and posts exhibited family crests, related a story, recounted an event, or explained a tradition—one could actually read the pictorial language of the carving. Known as genealogy poles, they were usually placed in front of the owner's home. Anyone passing by immediately knew the clan of the mother of the house. Other poles related the history of the clan through stories. From the carving, anyone could learn about an episode in the mythical past of the family that had influenced the destiny of their ancestors. Perhaps their starving ancestors had once been aided by a creature, or they had discovered fire. For example, the totem of the Kats house tells how Kats, a young warrior, ventured into the forest to stalk a grizzly bear. However, he fell in love with a female bear, who appeared to him as a beautiful woman. His adventure became a story of love, death, and the revenge of the clan.

The Tlingit carved memorial poles to honor a chief or beloved relative who had died. The ashes of the deceased were placed in a special compartment in the back of the pole. Carvers also made poles to mark an important event such as the birth of a child or a courageous deed of a warrior. Significant historic events could be recognized on a totem pole. When the United States purchased Alaska in 1867, people learned of

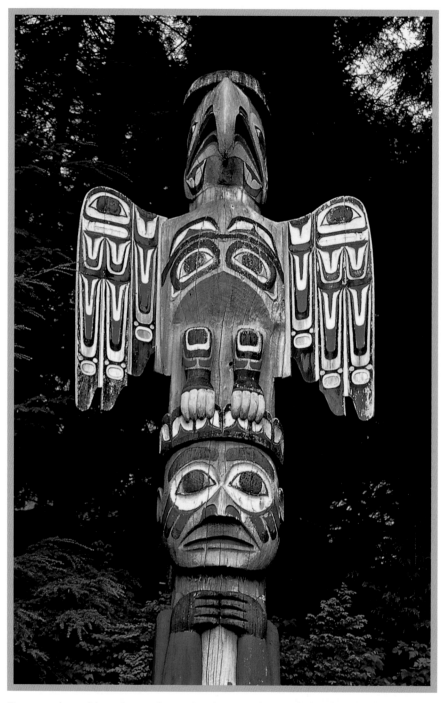

Totem poles told stories and acted as historical records for the Tlingit.

The People and Culture of the Tlingit

the Emancipation Proclamation, which had not only freed the Southern slaves but also ended slavery in Alaska. Chief Ebbits, whose family had lost its land and reputation on account of harboring escaped slaves from the Tlingit and Haida, erected an impressive pole in Abraham Lincoln's memory. Atop this 55-foot (17 m) pole is a likeness of the bearded president in tall black hat and coat.

Carving was—and still is—both an expression of the Tlingit way of life and an art form. Today, the works of Tlingit artists are prized by collectors and museums throughout the world.

How to Dress Like a Tlingit

During warm weather, men and women traditionally wore loincloths and skirts made of cedar bark. On rainy days, coastal people also put on waterproof basket caps made from twined spruce root and poncho-like raincoats made from spruce roots or cedar bark. Their clothing also included woven shirts, aprons, and leggings. They prominently displayed house and clan emblems on their clothing; the cone-shaped hats served as especially important crest objects. The Tlingit most likely learned the art of weaving from a group called the Tsimshian.

As winter approached, people switched to warm clothing made of tanned animal skins and wrapped themselves in blankets woven from cedar bark, goat wool, or dog hair. People living in the interior wore leather pants with moccasins attached and shirts made of tanned caribou or moose hides. During the harsh winter, they favored clothes made of animal pelts.

Chilkat blankets were the most impressive articles of clothing made by the Tlingit. In fact, Chilkat blankets were considered the most elaborate and highly valued textiles of any of the Native peoples of the Northwest coast. The blankets served as robes in ceremonies in which the dances were regarded as complex expressions of art. Although named after the Chilkat tribe, whose members came to excel at making the handicrafts, these blankets were originally woven by the Tsimshian. After they had mastered the craft, Tlingit women typically devoted one to five years to weaving mountain goat wool and strips of cedar bark to make a single blanket. Each of the intricately woven blankets featured a distinctive emblem of the clan. Worn over the shoulders as a cape, Chilkat blankets were symbols of wealth, and traditionally only clan leaders of great prestige could afford one. To give away a Chilkat blanket was a sign of great wealth, because only the very rich could afford to be so generous.

In the twentieth century, this art form was nearly lost as old weavers passed away. However, thanks to the dedicated efforts of several individuals, there are now many weavers, young and old, among the Tlingit and other coastal Native groups, who are making Chilkat blankets and teaching the craft to others.

The complicated technique of weaving the garment known as a Raven's Tail cape nearly vanished as well. These black and white capes with geometric and herringbone designs were not made for almost two centuries. Thanks to a cultural revival, the capes are now being woven throughout southeast Alaska. The techniques for making Chilkat blankets and Raven's

Tail capes are also used to weave other dance regalia, including leggings, medicine bags, purses, aprons, tunics, and shirts.

Today, Tlingit regalia often features a dancing robe known as a button blanket. Although it takes a long time to make these beautiful and expensive blankets, they are still more readily available than either Chilkat blankets or Raven's Tail capes. The Tlingit first made button blankets when they acquired felt from Russian traders. Usually red, black, or blue, the blankets are adorned with house or clan crests outlined or solidly beaded with buttons made of a seashell called mother-of-pearl. Worn at gatherings, like Chilkat blankets, these robes are a means for people to display their family heritage.

During ceremonies, men and women also wore headdresses. For men, these might be as simple as a headband or as elaborate as a hat carved from cedar wood. The clan crest was prominently featured on these hats, often trimmed with white ermine and inlaid with abalone shell. Women wore sailor-style hats modeled after those worn by Russian seamen. Made from the same felt as button blankets, these hats were adorned with beaded tassels.

To enhance their appearance, men and women also groomed their hair and adorned themselves with jewelry. They hung earrings from pierced ears and labrets from pierced noses. They wore bracelets and necklaces. They also painted their faces and tattooed their bodies. Many of these styles of dress and adornment, except for the labret, are still popular today. Through formal attire, the Tlingit continue not only to display their power, wealth, and heritage, but also to strengthen the social bonds within their community. In making and wearing a garment, they honor their ancestors and show respect toward other clans. The relationship of the garment maker and the wearer and of their respective clans is emphasized.

Traveling by Canoe, Trading

For the Tlingit, especially those living along the coast, canoes were the primary means of travel. The many styles included forked prow canoes, shallow river canoes, and ice-hunting canoes used in pursuing seals. Men also crafted small canoes with upturned ends to use when catching fish and hunting otter. Tlingit living inland sometimes paddled skin canoes, but most often they used small **dugouts** or rafts if they were not able to make their way on foot. On the coasts, the Tlingit constructed both large, oceangoing canoes, which could carry as many as sixty people, and small canoes, which men and women navigated down rivers and along the beach. Craftsmen usually made canoes during the winter months when they were not busy with hunting and fishing. Making a canoe required wisdom and great skill. Men first carefully selected the wood— cottonwood for a small canoe and red or yellow cedar for a large vessel. They preferred red cedar, but these trees grew mostly to the south in the territory of the Haida. Tlingit living in this area often harvested red cedars, and other Tlingit sometimes traded with the Haida for red cedar logs.

To make a small canoe, men first hollowed out the log with an adze, then filled the vessel with water heated with hot rocks. The steam and hot water softened the wood, which was then painstakingly shaped. The sides were gradually pulled and pushed apart and the ends were gracefully tapered. The canoe was then dried and smoked over a pitch fire to waterproof and blacken the wood. To make a large canoe, men skillfully hollowed out and joined separate logs to form a high prow and stem. The prow often featured carved figures, and the finished canoe was painted with crests and other clan symbols. The men made brushes from bear or porcupine hair and applied a waterproof paint made by blending minerals, salmon eggs, and chewed spruce gum.

Over land and water, the Tlingit established and maintained a vast trade network. This network linked the Northwest coast with the Athapaskan peoples who lived inland to the east and north, the Inuit of the northern coast and Siberia, and several tribes to the south, especially the Tsimshian and Haida. Over the course of several generations, privileged Tlingit chiefs came to enjoy hereditary rights to trade with Athapaskan leaders. They even married high-ranking women of these tribes to strengthen these relations. Trade routes followed river valleys, including the Taku, Stikine, and Alsek. These routes crossed mountain passes, notably Chilkat and Chilcoot, near present-day Haines, Alaska. Like many special activities, trading had religious significance. Traders prepared themselves by fasting, consulting a shaman, and then hosting a feast. Before departing on an expedition, they painted their faces to appear attractive to their trading partners. Goods were hauled up river by canoe, then carried by slaves in large baskets fitted with shoulder and forehead straps. Each backpack of a male slave held 100 or more pounds (45 kg) while each woman carried about 65 pounds (29 kg). Dogs labored with saddlebags weighing up to 25 pounds (11 kg). A good trader always brought along an elderly woman who shrewdly bargained for the best deals. Among the Tlingit's most valued imports were walrus ivory from the Inuit who lived near the Bering Sea, canoes from the Haida, and dentalia shells from other Native peoples in the south. Through trade, they also acquired slaves, furs, and skin garments in exchange for Chilkat blankets, seaweed, fish oil, and many other products. They traded for moose and caribou hides, leather thongs and sinews, and copper ore. They exchanged cedar baskets, fish oil, shells, and smoked seafood for finely sewn moccasins, birch wood bows wrapped with porcupine gut, and snowshoes. The Tlingit traded dentalia shells from Vancouver Island for rare items of copper and wood from the Inuit of Siberia and Alaska.

The Tlingit also regularly traded among themselves. Those living on the islands traded with mainland villages for dressed hides, rabbit and marmot skin blankets, moose-hide shirts, and skin trousers with moccasins attached. They sought cranberries preserved in oil, strawberry cakes, candlefish oil, horn spoons, woven blankets, and spruce root baskets. In exchange, the islanders offered sea otter pelts, dried venison, seal oil, dried seaweed, clams, mussels, and other sea creatures, along with dried fish, especially halibut, salmon, and herring.

When European traders arrived, many Tlingit became wealthy during the era of the fur trade. All

The People and Culture of the Tlingit

the Native peoples living in the interior longed for manufactured goods, including guns, gunpowder, shot, steel traps, knives, hatchets, and needles and thread, along with cloth and blankets. They also wanted staples such as flour, rice, and beans, as well as tobacco and molasses. During this time, the Tlingit were fairly effective in monopolizing trade in the region. They once journeyed as far as 300 miles (482 km) to destroy a post of the Hudson's Bay Company.

Life in the Tlingit kwan changed a lot thanks to trade with other nations. Being successful traders also helped them spread their culture to other people they encountered. These customs and ways of life were passed down to the following generations and honored as tradition. The Tlingit way of life from birth to death was heavily influenced by these cultural factors.

The Tlingit held all nature in high esteem.

CHAPTER FOUR

Show respect for others—each person has a special gift.

—LaVonne Rae Andrews, Tlingit

BELIEFS OF THE TLINGIT

The Tlingit people hold respect for traditions and their beliefs related to nature and their society. These have shaped their responses to interactions with foreign nations who have tried to impose outside beliefs on them. The Tlingit people have tried to maintain a hardline to their traditional beliefs at various times throughout history when the culture seemed to be waning.

The Tlingit used objects like these to carve totem poles, which depicted sacred and historical aspects of their culture.

The Sacred

The Tlingit revered animals and objects in nature. They believed they had souls like those of people. They respected animals that could bring misfortune or help, especially animals that gave their lives to sustain the families of hunters and fishermen. Before they hunted or fished, men purified themselves, and as they pursued game, they undertook special rituals. When they came home after an expedition, they offered thanks to the animals that had generously allowed themselves to be killed.

Every house and clan sought the protection of a shaman. Most were men, but women occasionally became shamans. It was believed that these powerful shamans possessed remarkable abilities to heal the body and the spirit. They not only effected cures but

This shaman wears traditional garb and holds a mask used in ceremonies.

Beliefs of the Tlingit

also influenced the weather, brought good fortune in hunting, foretold the future, exposed witches, and spoke with the dead. A shaman could be effective only if he were consulted in time and if another shaman was not working against him.

A shaman acquired his powers from the spirits he called upon in a sacred song. To remain pure and keep their powers strong, shamans often fasted and went without water. Neither a shaman nor his wife ever cut their hair. At the approach of his own death, a shaman sought out a younger relative to take his place. The young person became dizzy and ill until he or she accepted this obligation. The Tlingit held shamans in high regard. Yet, at one time, officers of the US Navy punished shamans by shaving their heads.

This chest was originally from Russia. Tlingit communities traded with the Russians for objects like these.

Celebrating with Potlatches

Native peoples of the Northwest, including the Tlingit, often came together for important celebrations known as potlatches. The term potlatch comes from the Nootka word *patshatl*, which means "giving" or "gift." In these feasts, nobles generously shared their wealth by feeding their guests and lavishing gifts on them. By accepting the food and gifts, the guests acknowledged the wealth and rank of the host. During the potlatch, the host family displayed their clan crests through songs and dances. Crests also adorned masks and other finely crafted objects—even the serving dishes. Afterward, the guests hosted their own potlatches to share what they had with their hosts and establish claims to property and rights to names.

All the coastal tribes of the Northwest held potlatches to mark key moments in the cycle of life. For example, the Tsimshian held a potlatch to mark the death of a leader, and the Haida celebrated the dedication of a chief's house and later his death with a potlatch.

The Tlingit held potlatches at three vital occasions—piercing the ears of noble children, funerals, and memorials when an heir assumed the position of leadership left by his mother's brother (uncle). During winter, houses also hosted potlatches to bring together spirits, ancestors, and the living to celebrate changes in rank and lives of family members. Partitions inside the house were removed to make a large room for guests who came from near and far. At these potlatches, guests respectfully called upon the spirits for help in feeding, clothing, and healing people.

The arrival of Europeans brought many devastating changes to the Native peoples of the Northwest that affected the tradition of potlatches. Hundreds of people, including many nobles, perished in

These dolls were toys belonging to Native children. They featured different Alaskan tribes, such as the Inuit and the Tlingit.

terrible epidemics of measles and smallpox for which the Native people had little or no resistance. Commoners then claimed the titles, rights, and wealth of the deceased nobles. Beginning in the 1830s, the Hudson's Bay Company offered valuable goods in exchange for furs, and a hardworking commoner could amass enough wealth to host a potlatch and lay claim to a high name. These commoners tended to use their newly acquired riches more as bribes than as gifts. People of different tribes also gathered in villages around forts and trading posts. This close everyday contact with new neighbors led to a cycle of extravagant, rival potlatches to establish the social positions of house, clan, and tribal chiefs among the Tlingit and other coastal people.

The potlatch came to be viewed as an elaborate game and a foolish extravagance corrupted by trade goods. Officials, missionaries, and Native converts in both the United States and Canada opposed the potlatch. They did not understand how people could devote years of their lives to amassing wealth only to give everything away. Potlatches were outlawed in both countries, but in the twenty-first century, the Tlingit are allowed to host these complex events that hold such deep meaning to them.

A Russian Orthodox priest named Innokentii converted many Tlingit.

Tlingit Religious Beliefs

The Tlingit religion is not practiced by most Tlingit. Most Tlingit have converted to Orthodox Christianity, which they got from Russian missionaries that were the first major European presence in their lands. Catholics and Protestants from America and Canada eventually found the Tlingit as well and converted them. Still, the traditions of the Tlingit are known and practiced today.

Tlingit people believe in the Creator Raven, who had a big part in the creation of the world. As read in chapter 1, one creation story tells of the Raven stealing the stars, the moon, and the sun.

The Tlingit also believe in a number of animal spirits, which can manifest their power through other animals and people. Tlingit are taught to respect the world of spirits and nature and to not let anything go to waste.

Storytelling and Legends

According to Tlingit beliefs, humans and animals are closely related. The animals who were once people fled into the forest and sea when Raven brought light to the world. They believe that animals may assume human form, as in one story in which a bear marries a woman. People, such as Salmon Boy, can also become animals. Of all the animals, it is thought that Bear and Raven are most like people. Walking on his hind legs, Bear hunts for the same foods as do people. With hand-like paws, he catches salmon and picks berries and nuts. Raven, moving cleverly between the human and the animal worlds, both generously helps people and plays tricks on them. He is also imbued with human flaws of selfishness and greed. These relationships between people and animals often emphasize the survival of the Tlingit, especially the vital task of acquiring food.

Here is one such story about how a Tlingit man and later his wife and children provided for others:

> Somewhere in the north, a young man from a noble family married a high-ranking young woman from a neighboring village. His mother-in-law lived with the newlyweds, and she disliked the youth. He seemed only interested in gambling and often stayed out very late at night. So, after every meal in the evening, the mother-in-law told the slaves, "Let the fire go out." She did not want her son-in-law to enjoy a warm meal when he finally stumbled home. When he at last arrived, late at night,

the mother-in-law whispered mockingly to her daughter, "I suppose he has been hard at work, felling a tree for me." Early the next morning the young man again left the clan house and did not return until well after dark. This happened every day, and his wife was dismayed. But she thought it was useless to say anything to him.

That summer all the people of the village, including the youthful gambler, journeyed to the river to fish for salmon. He did help in catching and drying the salmon, but afterwards he went into the woods and built a house beside a lake. With a stone ax, he then felled a large tree into the lake. He made wedges of hardwood with which to partially split the log, wedging a crossbeam in between to keep the two halves apart. He was making a trap because he had heard that a monster lived in the deep waters of that lake.

Baiting a hook and line with salmon, he waited for quite a while. When the line at last jiggled, he pulled rapidly. Caught on the hook, the monster rose to the surface between the two halves of the log. The young man then yanked the crossbeam so that the halves of the log sprang together and caught the monster's head.

The monster soon died and the young man dragged its body from the water. It had strong copper-like teeth and claws. The young man carefully skinned the monster with the claws and teeth attached to the shaggy hide. After the hide had properly cured, he crawled inside and slipped into the water. The hide swam away with him, carrying him to the monster's beautiful home under the lake. After he came up, the man hid the skin in a hole in a tree and went home, saying not a word about his adventure.

As winter approached, everyone went back to the village. For a while they had food, but the following spring there was a famine.

One morning, the man told his wife, "I am going away. If you hear a raven before I return, do not look for me anymore."

He retrieved the monster's skin and went to the beach not far from the village. Plunging into the water, he discovered that he could swim in the sea. He caught a king salmon. He carried the fish to the village and left it on the beach near the house where he lived with his wife and mother-in-law.

The next morning his mother-in-law arose early, walked outside, and found the salmon. She believed it had washed ashore. "I have found a fine big salmon!" she proudly announced. Her family cooked the salmon and shared its meat with everyone in the village, as was the custom of their people. The next evening, the young man caught two salmon and left them on the beach, where his mother-in-law found them. When he went to bed, the young man told his wife that he was getting those salmon, but not to say a word to anyone.

The third time that he brought salmon and his mother-in-law discovered them, she began to deeply ponder the situation. Her son-in-law now slept all day, and she chastised him, "If I did not pick up salmon, the whole village would be starving."

Afterwards, he and his wife laughed about her comments.

The next evening, he plunged into the sea and caught a very large halibut that he placed in front of his mother-in-law's house. When she found the fish, the mother-in-law was very pleased with herself. She now thought, "A spirit must be bringing luck to me."

The young man next caught a seal that he laid near the woman's house. He said nothing to his mother-in-law, although she belittled him more than ever. When a canoe landed at the village, she sneered, "I suppose my son-in-law has brought a load of seal."

That night, the mother-in-law pretended that a spirit visited and said to her, "I am the spirit that finds all this food for you." As she lay in bed, she told her husband, "Have a mask made for me, and let them name it Food Finding Spirit."

So, the next day her husband sent for the best carver in the village and had the mask made for her. He also had an apron made, fringed with puffin beaks and other fine ornaments. Wearing the mask, the mother-in-law walked around the village, shaking a rattle, and everyone believed that she was a powerful shaman. She talked often of her spirits, and the nobles spoke highly of her. However, she gave little food to her son-in-law and derided him more than ever, "Leave only a few scraps for Sleeping Man."

The young man kept saying to his wife, "Always listen for the ravens. If you hear a raven before I come you will know that something has happened to me." The young woman worried about her husband, and she was sad that her mother treated him so badly. The next day, the young man left a sea lion at the mother-in-law's house, and she was very proud. She invited all the people to a feast and boasted, "It has been this way from olden times. The chiefs of a village are always lucky."

Although she actually had not a single spirit, the mother-in-law believed that she was a great noble of her people. When the young man left a whale for her, she was especially haughty. She filled boxes with oil and all kinds of food that she sold to the people. But she shared very little with her daughter and son-in-law.

One night, the young man said to his wife, "If you find that I am dead in the skin, do not take me out of it. Put me and the skin in the place where I hid it, and you will get help."

This went on for a long time. The young man decided not to catch another whale because he had had such a hard time with the first one. He continued to bring food to his mother-in-law, who persisted in treating him spitefully. One day, he came upon two whales. He caught and tried to swim ashore with both of them. He worked all night, but just as he neared the beach, the raven called and he died at the edge of the water.

When his wife heard the cry of the raven, she quickly dressed, but she did not go outside. Then her mother walked out and found the two whales washed ashore with the monster lying between them. Everyone went down to the beach and when they saw the monster with fins on his back, long ears, and a very long tail, they cried, "That terrible monster must be the old woman's spirit."

Weeping loudly, the young woman then came down to the beach. She cried out to her lost husband.

The young woman turned on her mother and demanded, "Where is your spirit now? You are a storyteller. You have no spirit. That is why my husband died."

Everyone thought there was something wrong with her. They asked themselves, "What does that noble woman mean by saying that the monster is her husband?"

The young woman told her mother, "Is this your Food Finding Spirit? If so, how is it that your spirit died? Spirits never die. If this is your spirit, bring it to life again."

Then, as the young woman approached the monster, she said, "Some of you who are good and pure, come and help me."

As the people came near, they saw that the young woman's husband had died as he struggled to open the jaws of the monster—at the very moment that the raven had cried. They helped to place the body of the young man and the monster's skin in the hollow of a tree.

Thereafter, the old woman was so ashamed of herself that she would not set foot outside her house. She soon withered away and died.

Every evening, the young woman went to the foot of the tree and grieved tearfully for her lost husband. However, one night she noticed a ripple on the water and saw the monster in the lake. In the voice of her husband the monster called to her, "Come here, my beloved. Climb onto my back and hold tight." She did so, and together they swam down to the monster's beautiful home deep beneath the waters of the lake, where they live to this day. This monster and his wife now bring good fortune

Photographer Eadweard Muybridge most likely took this image of the Tlingit community in Tongass, Alaska, in 1868, when he visited the Tlingit village.

to anyone who sees them—as do the daughters who were born to them. These children are the Daughters of the Creek who live at the headwaters of every stream.

The Tlingit beliefs are shaped by how they view the world. Their worldview is expressed especially through their traditional stories. These stories serve to explain the relationships between humans and the forces of nature. Their beliefs draw from these relationships, from potlatches and gift giving to storytelling and oral traditions.

This statue features a Tlingit guide and commemorates the Klondike gold rush.

CHAPTER FIVE

*Our language is
like medicine.*

—Tlingit elder saying

OVERCOMING HARDSHIPS

Starting soon after the first modern explorers from all across the world came in contact with the Tlingit people, global culture started to blend in some areas and clash in others. A lot of nations and cultures were now beginning to share the same physical lands and boundaries. This cross-cultural existence created tension. Many lands that had been in the hands of Native nations for generations were being partitioned and sold to occupying nations as well as the rights to the resources therein. The Tlingit historically have both cooperated and resisted the various forces that collided with their way of life.

Tlingit Hardship Throughout History

Tlingit life started to change as soon as Europeans began to visit the coast of Alaska. In 1741, Russian explorer Aleksey Chirikov became the first European to touch upon the shores of southeastern Alaska. In 1775, Spaniard Bruno de Hezeta ventured into the region. He was followed by Frenchman Jean François de Galaup, Comte de La Pérouse in 1786, Italian Alejandro Malaspina in 1791, and Englishman George Vancouver in 1793. However, the Russians were the first to actually establish a settlement along the waters. In 1799, they constructed a military fort at Sitka. Three years later, Tlingit warriors under the leadership of Katlian (also spelled Katlyan) attacked and destroyed the post. However, in 1804, the Russians rebuilt the fort, which became the headquarters of the Russian-American Fur Company from 1808 to 1867. During this time, the Tlingit traded with the Russians for metal tools, cloth, and other goods, but otherwise tried to continue their ancestral way of life. Between 1835 and 1839, however, many people died in outbreaks of smallpox and other diseases. As they recovered from these sweeping epidemics, some Tlingit people converted to the Russian Orthodox religion.

Operating out of Canada, the Hudson's Bay Company acquired rights to trade in southeastern Alaska from the Russian-American Fur Company. Soon, goods manufactured in Europe began to pour into the region. Native people—including the Tlingit—eagerly sought these trade items, which included steel chisels and axes for carving totem poles and other wooden

This drawing, done by a Sioux Native American, shows the horror of the smallpox epidemics that affected many Native people.

objects. Dealing with both the Russian-American Fur Company and the Hudson's Bay Company, the Tlingit developed an extensive trade network in which they controlled much of the trade among the tribes living in the interior of Alaska. By the 1850s, they were trading as far south as Puget Sound in the present-day state of Washington, where they bartered with Americans for firearms and whiskey.

The Russians maintained a strong presence in Alaska until 1867. However, the great empire was staggering from its losses in the Crimean War and internal turmoil. In desperate need of funds, the czar, or ruler or Russia, agreed to sell Alaska to the United States for $7.2 million. At the time, many people in the United States objected to the deal, which they mockingly referred to as "Seward's Folly," after Secretary of State William H. Seward, who encouraged the purchase. The Tlingit bitterly opposed this sale as well. In their view, Alaska did not belong to Russia, and it had no right to sell the land to another country. They argued that if anyone owned Alaska, it was the Tlingit and the other Native peoples who lived there. The Tlingit protested the purchase and refused to submit to the United States. To assert authority over the Tlingit, the US Navy shelled the villages of Kake and Wrangell in 1869 and destroyed Angoon in 1882.

Through the remainder of the nineteenth century, waves of American soldiers, miners, and settlers came north to seek their fortune in gold mines, fishing, and other enterprises. They mistreated the Tlingit and other Alaskan Natives. Although they had lived there for thousands of years, Alaskan Natives were treated as

Chilkat Tlingit porters pose with a miner (*right*) on the Chilkoot Trail in 1897.

inferior to the newcomers. They were allowed few or no rights. Although the Tlingit held aboriginal title to the territory, they were not permitted to file land claims in a gold rush near Juneau in 1880. When commercial fishing and canning operations were established in the 1870s and 1880s, the Tlingit received lower wages than other

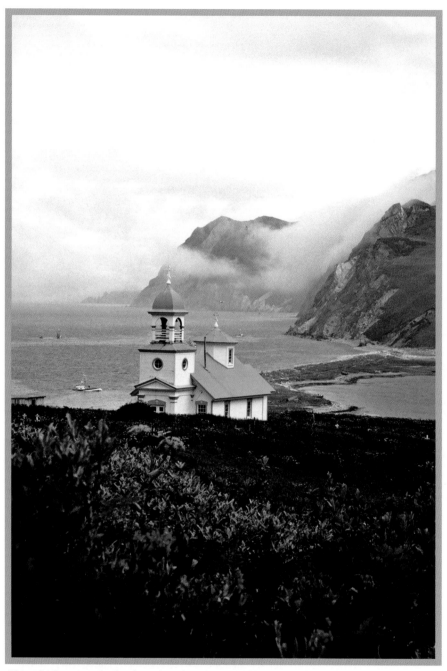

This old Russian Orthodox church sits on Kodiak Island, Alaska.

The People and Culture of the Tlingit

workers—if they could get a job at all. In 1897–1898, the Klondike gold rush brought more jobs and money to the region, but Alaska Natives benefitted little.

Changing Way of Life

In the latter years of the nineteenth century, the Tlingit way of life was challenged by missionaries from the United States and Canada, especially Presbyterians, who established churches in their midst. Most coastal Tlingit had long since converted to the Russian Orthodox faith after the smallpox epidemic that raged from 1835 to 1839. However, Presbyterian missionaries now criticized them for using the Russian alphabet and expressing the beliefs of the Russian Orthodox religion. Many other Protestant and Catholic missionaries also descended upon the Tlingit. Competing for the souls of the Tlingit, these missionaries tried to impose their own version of Christianity on the Native people and to extinguish all ancestral beliefs and customs. The bawdy cry of Raven was silenced, as traditional stories gave way to those of a great flood or other stories drawn from the Bible.

By the turn of the century, many Tlingit had also abandoned a way of life based on hunting, fishing, and gathering. Many villages were completely deserted as people moved to cities to seek jobs in canneries. Some went as far as British Columbia looking for work. Many journeyed even farther away to the sprawling fields of eastern Washington where they picked hops. The Tlingit held few, if any, potlatches, which were no longer considered significant to families and communities. The dances, rituals, and art objects related to these great celebrations were nearly forgotten. The Tlingit sold many of their cherished objects to museums and collectors—or the priceless ancestral objects were stolen. However, a few villages resisted these overwhelming changes and struggled desperately to continue the ways of their ancestors.

Preserving the Tlingit Language

One of the most powerful links to a culture and people is language. As the Tlingit spread northward, their language came to vary somewhat from one region to the next, which made it more difficult to preserve. As noted by a well-known authority on Tlingit culture, Frederica de Laguna, "There are slight differences in pronunciation between the quick-speaking southerners and the more drawling, louder northerners." Among the northerners, especially along the Gulf coast, the sounds are pronounced farther back in the throat.

Here are some examples of the Tlingit language based on the *English-Tlingit Dictionary*, compiled by Constance Naish and Gillian Story. Some letters are pronounced as in English, but Tlingit is a very complex language with eight vowels and forty-three consonants. The following examples have been simplified, but offer an idea of how to pronounce a number of Tlingit words.

The vowels are generally pronounced as follows:

a	as in was
e	as in ten
i	as in hit
u	as in push
aa	as in father

Two Tlingit women display button blankets and drums.

ei as in v*ei*n

ee as in s*ee*k

oo as in m*oo*n

The consonants have many variations with no equivalents in English, and their diacritic marks have been omitted in this brief vocabulary. Note, however, that the Tlingit x is pronounced something like *sh* but farther back in the mouth, like the *ch* in the German word *ach*. Fourteen Tlingit sounds are made with an accompanying glottal stop, or catch-in-the-breath sound. These are represented by an apostrophe (') after the letter.

People

at	aunt (father's sister)
tlak'w	aunt (mother's sister)
honxw	brother, older
keek	brother, younger
ut k'utsk'oo	child
see	daughter
eesh	father
duchxun	grandchild
leelk'w	grandparent
xox	husband
tlah	mother
shutx	sister, older
keek	sister, younger
yeet	son
sunee	uncle (father's brother)
kak	uncle (mother's brother)
shut	wife

Parts of the Body

jigei	arm
gok	ear
wak	eye
x'oos	foot, leg
jin	hand
shuh	head
teix'	heart
x'eh	mouth
lidex'	neck
loh	nose
dook	skin

Natural World

geey	bay
eek	beach
gil'	cliff
as gootoo	forest
sit'	glacier
t'eex'	ice
xatl	iceberg
x'at'	island
tl'utk	land, earth
tleiyun	mainland
shah	mountain
eil'	ocean
heen	river
gagaan	sun
shanux	valley
x'as	waterfall

Sky and Weather

kogwas'	fog
kuxwan	frost
dis	moon
gees'ook	Northern Lights
seew, soow	rain
takw eetee	spring
kotan	summer
yeis	fall
takw	winter
goos'	sky, cloudy
xats'	sky, clear
kuxluheen, kukluheen	snow, wet
dleit kuketsk	snow, dry
kotx uyunuhah	star
gugan	sun

Mammals

s'eek	bear, black
xoots	bear, brown
wutsix	caribou
keitl	dog
dzisk'w	moose
kooshdah	otter, land
gux	rabbit
junwoo	sheep, mountain
kunuls'ak	squirrel
gooch	wolf

Thanks to the work and perseverance of the Tlingit against hardship, their culture has persisted to this day.

Modern efforts have revitalized lost or unpracticed traditions and helped secure teaching of the language for newer generations. The hardships imposed on them by foreign nations and nature have affected the Tlingit in many ways. The challenge of such a smaller world has occasionally proved difficult for the Tlingit through the many nations that have sought to use the land the Tlingit live on. Throughout these hardships, the Tlingit culture has not lost its connection to nature.

Juneau, Alaska, was built on Tlingit lands.

We have only uncovered a tiny portion of the way our ancient people used to do things ... You have untied it for us. That is why we will open it again, this container of wisdom left in our hands.

—George Davis, 1980

THE NATION'S PRESENCE NOW

The Tlingit are currently one of a number of Native nations recognized by the countries who draw their borders around them, therefore maintaining their sovereignty. Many Tlingit seek to preserve their heritage and tradition while fighting for equal treatment and rights from those around them. There have been many organizations started and joined by the Tlingit to ensure their voices can continue to be heard.

In 1740, there were at least 10,000 Tlingit living in what is now southeastern Alaska and

Canada. Despite widespread epidemics and other hardships, by the 1990s, there were about 14,000 Tlingit in the United States and 1,200 in Canada. Many people continue to live in ancestral villages, but others now make their home in Ketchikan, Juneau, and other cities in the Northwest. Major Tlingit villages include Yakutat, Hoonah, Klukwan, Angoon, Kake, Craig, and Klawock. As of 2016, there was an estimated Tlingit population of over 16,000.

Alaska Native Brotherhood and Alaska Native Sisterhood

In 1912, the Alaska Native Brotherhood (ANB) was founded by Presbyterian Natives who sought rapid assimilation along with economic opportunities, land rights, and an end to discrimination to their people. Soon after, the Alaska Native Sisterhood (ANS) was established with similar goals. (However, in the late 1960s, both organizations reversed their positions and came to favor the preservation of Tlingit language and customs.) In 1924, Native peoples were allowed to vote in Alaska. But most Natives, including the Tlingit, were still considered members of a lower social and economic class. They remained segregated from other Alaskans. Despite repeated efforts by the Tlingit, schools in Alaska were not integrated until 1949.

The Tlingit Central Council

After the Indian Reorganization Act was extended by Congress in 1936 to include Alaska, a few villages incorporated and supported themselves through small industries. Following World War II, the Tlingit also

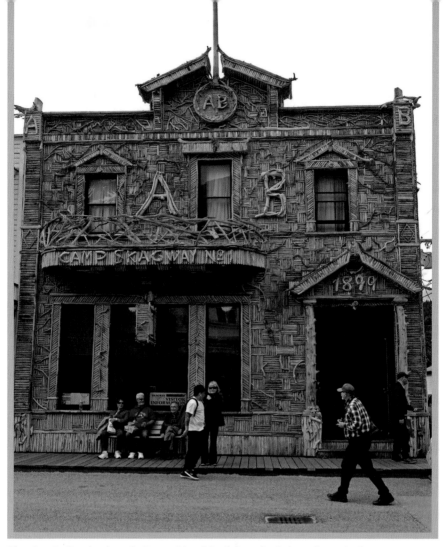

The Arctic Brotherhood, Camp No. 1 building, built by miners in Sagway, Alaska, in 1899, is a reminder of the area's gold rush history.

sought to reclaim a portion of their land. Joining with the Haida, who have communities at the southern tip of the Alaskan panhandle, they established the Central Council of Tlingit and Haida, which in 1968 settled a land claim for $7.5 million. According to the preamble of the council's constitution, its purpose is to "preserve their identity as Indian tribes and the identity and culture of their members and their descendants as Indian people [and to] provide for the exercise of their tribal sovereignty." Today, the Central Council of the Tlingit and Haida Indian Tribes (CCTHITA) is the federally recognized tribal organization of the Tlingit in Alaska. The council is made up of delegates elected from communities in southeastern Alaska and other communities.

The CCTHITA is responsible for a number of initiatives including an economic development program to help create jobs in southeast Alaska, a cultural resources program that repatriates objects of cultural importance, and a business development program that helps Tlingit members get loans.

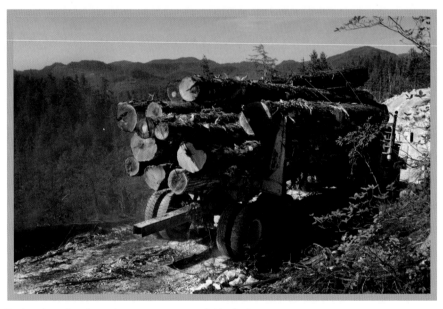

Today, logging is an important part of Alaska's economy.

The Sealaska Corporation

In 1971, according to terms of the Alaska Native Claims Settlement Act, twelve regional corporations, including

The People and Culture of the Tlingit

Sealaska, which encompasses Tlingit territory, and about two hundred village corporations were established. The Tlingit and other Native peoples of Alaska also received nearly $1 billion and title to 44 million acres (18 million hectares) in exchange for giving up ancestral claims to all other lands. In the early 1970s, the Sealaska Corporation received 280,000 acres (113,311 ha) of timberland and $200 million. Each village received surface land rights while the corporation was granted subsurface rights. These corporations are now involved in logging, fishing, and development of the land. These initiatives have led to an economic resurgence among the Tlingit and other Native Alaskans.

Other Tlingit Organizations

No more than four hundred Tlingit ever lived inland. The Inland Tlingit came into greater contact with outsiders in the 1940s when the Alaska Highway opened. In the 1960s, radio and television brought more rapid changes. Today, most young people on the coast and interior speak only English. The Teslin (Yukon) and the Taku River (British Columbia) Tlingit are recognized by the government of Canada. The Teslin Tlingit are now part of the Carcross Tagish First Nation. The Teslin Tlingit Council, as part of the Daxa Nation, has three reserves in the southwest of Teslin in Canada. In the early 1990s, the population totaled 482 people living in 119 households. Today, they are a self-governing First Nation. Since the late 1940s, the Department of Indian Affairs has required elections for leadership positions. Clan leaders include a chief and five counselors. Tlingit children attend schools managed by the nation or the province. There are other facilities on the reserves, including administration buildings and a longhouse, clinic, and recreation center.

Despite their often remote locations, most Tlingit villages now have electric service, internet, and satellite television. Every village has an elementary school and at least one church. A few also have a high school. Most children, however, have to travel to a larger city to attend high school. People still follow the clan system, although its influence has faded in recent years. Now Christian, most Tlingit people, especially those living in cities, have abandoned traditional ways. Very few people can speak Tlingit, although the language is now being taught in the schools. The ANB and ANS are also working to renew the traditional culture of the Tlingit. Important ceremonies—notably potlatching, singing, dancing, and crest arts—have also enjoyed a revival in recent years. A vigorous political, economic, and cultural revival is now underway, and the Tlingit are determined that their children will have a brighter future.

Celebrations

Tlingit gatherings and celebrations are one of the biggest ways that the Tlingit are able to express their culture and voice. The Hà Kus Teyea Celebration is one that takes place every year where participants partake in traditional Tlingit activities. There is a traditional lake crossing in a canoe, followed by a greeting ceremony and the lighting of the Celebration Fire. There is a parade, food vendors, and cultural demonstrations.

Another such event is the Sealaska Celebration, held every two years in June. It occurs over four days where

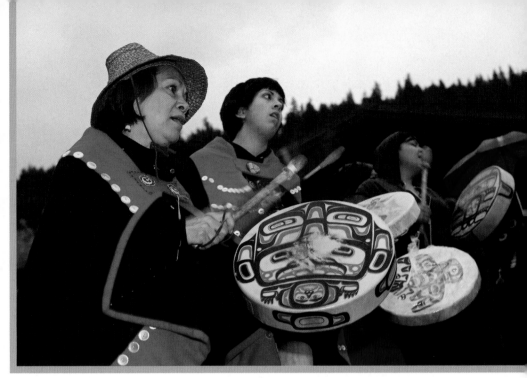

The Tlingit celebrate their ancestry with singing, dancing, and tradition.

the streets of Juneau, Alaska, are flooded with people. The event draws over five thousand people, two thousand of which are dancers and performers. It was started in 1982, but it represents the strongest revival of Tlingit traditions with emphasis put back on the two moieties of Raven and Eagle tribes and reciprocity in the giving and hosting as dictated by tradition.

Modern living and amenities are currently available to the Tlingit people, despite many living in more remote areas of the world. This has afforded an avenue for Tlingit people to communicate and share ideas as well as being exposed to other ones. Though the Tlingit language is not spoken by very many people, the language is still alive and available to more people thanks to the work of activist and nonprofit organizations and the people who carry out their missions.

Tommy Joseph, a Tlingit member, is renowned for his carving abilities.

CHAPTER SEVEN

The sense of satire is a continuation of stuff that has been going on for thousands of years.

—Larry McNeil,
Tlingit photographer

FACES OF THE TLINGIT

People are recognized for their achievements and things they do that stand out. These Tlingit are notable for their contributions to both Tlingit society and outside societies. Key figures from the Tlingit that have had a positive impact on the world and shaped the future include public servants, soldiers, leaders, educators, anthropologists, activists, and chiefs. The following significant individuals list themselves among the Tlingit people.

William G. Demmert Jr. (1934–2010), university professor and administrator, was born in Klawock, Alaska. He graduated from Seattle Pacific College and then taught at Forks, Washington, from 1960 to 1964. In 1965, he moved to Fairbanks, Alaska, where he lived until moving back to his hometown in 1968. There, he was chief administrator of the public school system until 1970. Meanwhile, in 1969, Demmert, who is of Tlingit and Dakota Sioux descent, was invited to attend the First Convocation of American Indian Scholars. As a result of this meeting, Demmert helped to found the National Indian Educational Association, and became one of the original directors.

While attending Harvard University from 1970 to 1973, he worked for the passage of the Indian Education Act of 1972. He also joined the US Department of Education as an official in Native American education in 1972 and received his doctorate from Harvard the following year. During his lifetime, he published many articles in the field of education and taught at many prominent universities, including the University of Alaska, Stanford University, the University of Washington, and Harvard University. He also held positions in several federal agencies and programs, such as the Indian Nations at Risk Force, dedicated to improving the quality of education for Native American children. He died in 2010.

Katlian (Katlyan) (active early 1800s), a Tlingit leader born and raised in the coastal village of Sitka, led the Tlingit in several conflicts against Russian traders and colonists in southeastern Alaska. The Russians arrived

Members of the modern-day Tlingit tribe hold a Raven helmet that belonged to and was worn into battle by Katlian.

on the Aleutian Islands after Vitus Bering undertook an exploratory voyage in 1741 and confirmed that Alaska was a body of land separate from Asia. The Russians forced the Aleuts to help catch sea otters, whose fur was highly prized. Gradually moving eastward, the Russians established a fort near Sitka in 1799. Three years later, Katlian led an attack on the fort and drove the Russians from Sitka. Katlian and his men held the fort for two years until a force of about 120 Russians and 1,000 Aleuts returned with cannons. They bombarded the fort and the soldiers attacked. Katlian and his men retreated, but they remained hostile to the Russians. In 1805, Katlian attacked a post at Yakutat. The traders appealed to the Russian navy for protection, and in 1818, a Russian warship began to patrol Sitka Harbor. However, Katlian and other Tlingit warriors continued their hostilities, which became one of the reasons the Russians decided to sell Alaska to the United States in 1867.

Elizabeth W. Peratrovich (Kaaxgal-aat) (1911–1958), a prominent civil rights leader, was born in Petersburg, Alaska, where she attended elementary school. She went to high school in Ketchikan and then attended Western College of Education in Bellingham, Washington. In 1931, she married Roy Peratrovich. Ten years later, they moved back to Alaska with their family. Elizabeth and her husband became active in the Alaska Native Brotherhood and Alaska Native Sisterhood, organizations that sought to gain civil rights for Native peoples. When the Peratroviches moved to Juneau, Elizabeth was grand camp (chapter) president of the ANS and Roy was grand-president of the regional ANB.

The organizations had already helped Alaska Natives gain the right to vote in 1922. Yet Native children were not allowed to attend public schools in Juneau, and the ANB sued to integrate the school district. At that time, the Peratroviches also encountered signs that read "No Natives Allowed" and "No Dogs or Indians Allowed." They were outraged when they were not allowed to purchase a home in a neighborhood they liked. The Peratroviches confronted the Alaskan territorial legislature with these issues of discrimination. They lobbied daily until an anti-discrimination bill

The People and Culture of the Tlingit

Elizabeth Peratrovich was an active member of the Tlingit community, dedicated to promoting equality among Native people.

was proposed. Elizabeth offered vivid testimony that swayed the legislature to vote 11–5 in favor of the bill outlawing discrimination in housing, public accommodations, and restaurants in Alaska.

On February 16, 1945, the act was signed into law. It was the first anti-discrimination law in the United States. While Alaska was still a territory, it made significant advances in civil rights in large part because of the efforts of Elizabeth and Roy Peratrovich. In 1988, February 16 was officially declared Elizabeth W. Peratrovich Day in Alaska. Elizabeth died of cancer at the age of forty-seven, yet she is remembered every year on this date.

This sun totem can be seen on Chief Shakes Island in Alaska.

Shakes (Shaikes) (active 1800s) was the hereditary name of an important family and several Tlingit chiefs who lived on Wrangell Island in what is now known as the Alexander Archipelago of southeastern Alaska. The name Shakes was first noted by the 1841–1842 expedition of Sir George Simpson. The Shakes became one of the wealthiest and most powerful families because of the fur trade on their island and up the Stikine River on the Alaska mainland. They traded with the Russians and the English. After the United States purchased Alaska in 1867, missionaries came

The People and Culture of the Tlingit

to Wrangell Island, but Chief Shakes rejected all their efforts to convert him. Shakes received assurances of financial assistance from the United States for schools and economic development, but the promises were never fulfilled. In the early 1900s, the last chief of the Shakes lineage established a museum with an impressive collection of art objects of Native peoples of the Northwest coast. The last Chief Shakes died in 1944.

Rosita Worl (Yeidiklatsokw) (1937–), anthropologist, activist, and educator, was born in Petersburg, Alaska, and raised in Haines, Juneau, and Petersburg. Her traditional home village is Klukwan on the Chilkat River, not far from Haines. She attended a mission boarding school in Haines for three years, then after returning home, she learned Tlingit traditions from her mother and grandparents. Worl also learned a great deal from her mother's dedicated activities as a union organizer in canneries. After graduating from Juneau High School, Worl attended Alaska Methodist University where she graduated magna cum laude in 1972. She earned a master's degree in social anthropology from Harvard University in 1975. She received a Ford Foundation fellowship to pursue her studies, including postgraduate work, from 1972 to 1975. She has since been a research anthropologist and co-curator of the "Tlingit Clans and Corporations" exhibition at the National Museum of Natural History. She has also worked on several state projects in Alaska on behalf of Native peoples.

As an anthropologist, Worl has worked in the field on many arduous projects in Alaska and Canada. Her

Rosita Worl in September 2013

work with the Inuit of the far north helped to preserve their right to hunt whales. She also undertook research on the impact of oil development on the Native peoples of Alaska. She then moved to Anchorage, where she worked as an assistant professor of anthropology at the University of Alaska. As a member of the Alaska Native Brotherhood and the Alaska Native Sisterhood, Worl has worked for the social welfare and civil rights of Alaska Natives. She has been one of the individuals responsible for the cultural renaissance of the Tlingit. She has served on the boards of the

Klukwan Heritage Foundation, the Alaska State Arts Council, the Traditional Native Arts Panel, and the Folk Arts Panel of the National Endowment for the Arts.

Worl has received several awards for her work, including the Alaska Press Club Award for Excellence for Return of Native Artifacts, 1987–1988. She is also active in Keepers of the Treasures, Alaska Natives and Native Hawaiians, and she has served as vice-chair of the Sealaska Heritage Foundation. Her research and writing emphasize the traditions of the Tlingit. Among her essays is "History of Southeastern Alaska Since 1867," published in the *Handbook of North American Indians, Northwest Coast*, Volume 7, by the Smithsonian Institution Press. When asked how she maintains such a daunting schedule, Worl responded, "I require very little sleep."

The Tlingit people have a culture that is preserved thanks to outspoken figures who cherish the traditions and heritage. By making a positive impact in the world, they are also creating and preserving pieces of Tlingit history and values. As they are identified by both their cultural heritage and their achievements, they reflect positively on their places of origin.

CHRONOLOGY

1741 Russian explorers enter the coastal waters of the Tlingit and other Alaskan Natives.

1786 First confirmed encounter of the Tlingit with Europeans when Jean François de Galaup, Comte de La Pérouse, a French explorer, enters Lituya Bay and stays in Alaska for three months.

1804 The Battle of Sitka occurs between Russians and the Tlingit in response to the increased hostilities between the two sides. The result of the battle displaces many Tlingit northward.

1808–1867 Russians establish trading settlements along the coast of Alaska.

1835–1839 Epidemics of smallpox and other diseases sweep through Tlingit communities.

1867 At the initiative of William H. Seward, the United States purchases Alaska from Russia for $7,200,000.

1884 The Organic Act is passed by Congress, allowing for a basic form of government in Alaska.

1887 The General Allotment Act, also known as the Dawes Act, divides reservation lands into small tracts that are allocated to individual tribal members. The remaining land is sold by the government.

1897 The Act of June 6, 1897, prohibits the use of native subsistence fish traps in Alaska. The Klondike gold rush begins on July 6. In less than two months, thirty thousand men pour into the territory.

1900 Congress enacts the Carter Code, which extends the civil laws of Oregon Territory to Alaska.

1902 President Theodore Roosevelt establishes the Tongass National Forest. Eventually, protected lands include nearly 16 million acres (6.5 million hectares) in southeast Alaska.

1906 The Native Allotment Act grants 160 acres (65 ha) of public land to adult Native peoples. Few tracts were awarded, however, because the Bureau of Land Management would not recognize subsistence use of the land for hunting and fishing as proof of "use and occupancy."

1912 Alaska becomes a territory with a two-house legislature. The Alaska Native Brotherhood holds its first organizational meeting. Peter Simpson is elected as the first president of the organization.

1922 Voting rights of Alaska Natives are affirmed when W. L. Paul Sr. successfully defends Charlie Jones, who is charged with illegal voting.

1924 Alaskan Natives become US citizens. The Alexander Fish Bill outlaws subsistence fishing in southeast Alaska.

1926 W. L. Paul Sr. is the first Alaska Native elected to the territorial house of representatives.

1929 In court proceedings, W. L. Paul Sr. establishes the right of Native children to attend public schools. An ANB convention at Haines resolves to pursue the Tlingit and Haida land claims.

1934 The Indian Reorganization Act allows greater independence for Native peoples, but Alaska is excluded in the law.

1935 The Jurisdictional Act creates a governing body for the Tlingit and Haida.

1936 At the request of the ANB, the Indian Reorganization Act is amended to include Alaska.

1939 The ANB organizes the Central Council and elects Andrew Hope as president. However, the US Department of the Interior challenges the legitimacy of the organization and another election is held at the 1941 convention.

1945 After many years of effort by ANB, the territorial legislature passes the Anti-Discrimination Act.

1946 Mt. Edgecumbe High School opens in Sitka, a small community in southeast Alaska. Many future Native leaders attend this Native boarding school. Frank Peratrovich, an Alaska Native, is elected president of the Alaska senate.

1949 Alaska schools are integrated.

1959 On January 3, Alaska becomes the forty-ninth state. One of the first laws passed by the new Alaska state legislature outlaws the use of fish traps.

1965 The Central Council amends the Jurisdictional Act of 1935, thereby recognizing the council as the governing body of the Tlingit and Haida, and reducing the authority of the Bureau of Indian Affairs (BIA).

1966 On October 18, the first meeting of the Alaska Federation of Natives is held in Anchorage.

1968 The US Court of Claims awards the Tlingit and the Haida people $7.5 million for lands taken to form the Tongass National Forest and Glacier Bay National Monument. Funds are not actually awarded to the Central Council until 1970.

1971 On December 18, the Alaska Native Claims Settlement Act takes effect.

1972 The Indian Education Act is passed.

1978 The Indian Child Welfare Act is passed by Congress.

1982 For the first time, the Tlingit, Haida, and Tsimshian nations come together in a celebration of their Native cultures.

1984 The Andrew Hope Building is completed and becomes the headquarters of the Central Council.

1993 The Central Council is removed from the list of federally recognized tribes.

1994 US Congress restores the Central Council to the list of federally recognized tribes.

2000 An Alaska Airlines jet crashes near Los Angeles. Eighty-eight people die, including some prominent leaders.

2004 The Tlingit living in Icy Strait Point in Hoonah, Alaska, have the first cruise ship land on their shores.

2004 At the Bicentennial of the Battle of Sitka, the descendants of both sides of the conflict hold a traditional Tlingit "crying ceremony" for the first time officially to grieve fallen ancestors. The next day the Kiks.ádi host a formal reconciliation ceremony to put away two centuries of grieving.

GLOSSARY

adze A cutting tool shaped like an axe that has an arched blade at a right angle to the handle. It is used for both shaping the wood and cutting it.

bentwood boxes Traditional boxes made by Native peoples of the North American west coast that are often made of a single piece of wood that is steamed and then bent to form a box.

canoe A sailing vessel, also called a dugout, made of red cedar with a high prow, often emblazoned with the crest of its owner.

clan A group of lineages, or families, descended from common ancestors.

clan house A large dwelling in which several related families from the same clan live together.

commoner One of the classes of people in Tlingit society who did not own houses or other valuable property.

dugout A boat made by hollowing out a large log.

kwan Groups of people living in the same geographic area.

lineage A family line; a group of people descended from a common ancestor.

matrilineal Tracing descent through the mother's side of the family.

moieties The two halves of society; the Tlingit moieties are Raven and Wolf (sometimes called Eagle in the north).

nobles People belonging to the highest social class of the Tlingit.

potlatch A ceremonial feast held on special occasions in which the host gives away many valuable presents.

roe A mass of fish eggs.

shaman Mostly men who were believed to possess a number of abilities including healing, influencing the weather, good hunting fortune, predicting the future, and communicating with the dead. As a symbol of their power, they never cut their hair.

smokehouse A building in which fish or meat is preserved by smoking and drying.

spawn Laying and fertilizing a large number of eggs, said of fish.

tobacco pellets Small bits of tobacco mixed with cedar or spruce gum that were sucked on for flavor.

totem pole A pole carved from red cedar on which people displayed their crests and related family histories.

BIBLIOGRAPHY

Beasley, Richard A. *Tlingit Wood Carving: How to Carve a Tlingit Mask*. Juneau, AK: Sealaska Heritage Institute, 2009.

Edwards, Keri. *Dictionary of the Tlingit*. Juneau, AK: Sealaska Heritage Insititute, 2011.

Gmelch, Sharon Bohn. *The Tlingit Encounter with Photography*. Philadelphia, PA: University of Pennsylvania Museum of Archaeology and Anthropology, 2008.

Johnson, Michael, and J. Burkinshaw. *Native Tribes of the North and Northwest Coast*. Milwaukee, WI: World Almanac Library, 2004.

Kan, Sergei. *Symbolic Immortality: The Tlingit Potlatch of the Nineteenth Century*. 2nd ed. Seattle, WA: University of Washington Press, 2016.

Peratrovich, Roy A. *Little Whale: A Story of the Last Tlingit War Canoe*. Fairbanks, AK: University of Alaska Press, 2016.

Swanton, John R. *The Tlingit Indian Language*. Seattle, WA: Shorey Book Store, 1971.

Thornton, Thomas F. *Being and Place Among the Tlingit*. Seattle, WA: University of Washington Press, 2007.

Waller, Dennis. *Otter Tales: Stories of the Land Otter Man of the Tlingit*. Seattle, WA: CreateSpace, 2014.

The People and Culture of the Tlinglit

FURTHER INFORMATION

Want to know more about the Tlingit? Check out these websites, videos, and organizations.

Websites

History of Hoonah

http://www.cityofhoonah.org/community/page/history-hoonah

Visit this page to view an informative section about the town of Hoonah and the Huna Tlingit.

Tlingit

http://www.omniglot.com/writing/tlingit.htm

This article about the Tlingit provides examples of the written form of the language.

Words from the Circle

http://www.nativevillage.org/Libraries/Quotes/Native%20American%20Quotes%208%20.htm

This website provides quotes from different nations, including the Tlingit.

Videos

Tlingit History of Southeast Alaska

https://www.youtube.com/watch?v=uiTUsTpl8wc

Learn about Tlingit history from modern members of the Tlingit.

Tlingit Past and Present

https://www.youtube.com/watch?v=HhdhNso86tk

This short video outlines the history of the Tlingit.

Tlingit Totem Poles

https://www.youtube.com/watch?v=YvTKyV6G414

Watch this presentation on Tlingit totem poles.

Organizations

Alaska Inter-Tribal Council

445 E. 5th Ave.

Anchorage, AK 99501

(907) 563-9334

http://www.aitc.org

Alaska Native Heritage Center

8800 Heritage Center Drive

Anchorage, AK 99504

(907) 330-8000

http://www.alaskanative.net

Alaska State Museum
395 Whittier St.
Juneau, AK 99801
(907) 465-2901
http://museums.alaska.gov

Central Council Tlingit & Haida Indian Tribes of Alaska
320 W. Willoughby Ave., Suite 300
Juneau, AK 99801
(907) 586-1432
http://www.ccthita.org

Sealaska Corporation
One Sealaska Plaza, Suite 400
Juneau, AK 99801
(907) 586-1512
http://www.sealaska.com

Sheldon Jackson Museum
104 College Drive
Sitka, AK 99835
(907) 747-8981
http://museums.alaska.gov/sheldon_jackson/sjhome.html

Taku River Tlingit First Nation
PO Box 132
Atlin, BC V0W 1A0
Canada
(250) 651-7900
http://trtfn.com

Teslin Tlingit Council
PO Box 133
Teslin, Yukon Territory Y0A 1B0
Canada
(867) 390-2532
http://www.ttc-teslin.com

Yakutat Tlingit Tribe
PO Box 416
Yakutat, AK 99689
(907) 784-3238
http://yak-tatkwaan.com

INDEX

Page numbers in **boldface** are illustrations. Entries in **boldface** are glossary terms.

The People and Culture of the Tlingit

ABOUT THE AUTHORS

Erika Edwards has written several children's books and continues to grow and learn as a writer and editor. Edwards is of Iroquois, and more specifically, Mohawk and Cayuga ancestry. She values indigenous language, food, and culture. It is important to her that these aspects of her heritage remain available for generations to come. She currently resides in Niagara Falls, New York.

Raymond Bial has published more than eighty books—most of them photography books—during his career. His photo-essays for children include *Corn Belt Harvest, Amish Home, Frontier Home, The Underground Railroad, Portrait of a Farm Family, Cajun Home,* **and** *Where Lincoln Walked.*

As with his other work, Bial's deep feeling for his subjects is evident in both the text and illustrations. He travels to tribal cultural centers, photographing homes, artifacts, and surroundings and learning firsthand about the national lifeways of these peoples.

The emeritus director of a small college library in the Midwest, he lives with his wife and three children in Urbana, Illinois.